#Superlativa_001
Inspirational

YOUCANPRINT SELF-PUBLISHING

The brandless luxury superlativa ®

club@superlativa.it

superlativa

Titolo | Superlativa Inspirational #001

ISBN | 978-88-93217-35-4

Youcanprint Self-Publishing
Via Roma, 73 - 73039 Tricase (LE) - Italy
www.youcanprint.it
info@youcanprint.it
Facebook: facebook.com/youcanprint.it
Twitter: twitter.com/youcanprintit

"People don't take trips... trips take people"

(John Steinbeck, *Travels with Charley: In Search of America*)

"*The real voyage of discovery consists not in seeking new landscapes, but in having new eyes*"

(Marcel Proust)

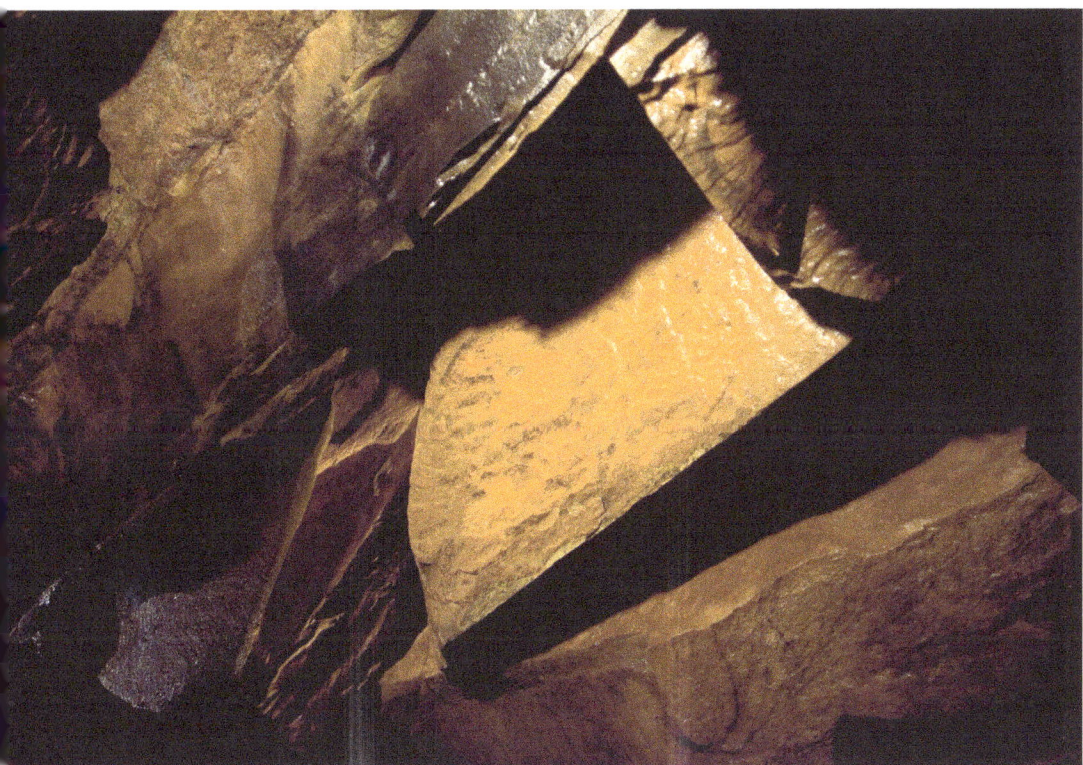

"Travelling is like dreaming: the difference is that, on waking, not everyone remembers the journey, whereas everyone vividly preserves the memory of where they have stayed"

(Edgar Allan Poe)

"The journey never ends. Only travelers end. When the traveler is sitting on the sand of the beach and said: There is nothing to see , he knew that it was not true. We need to see what we haven't seen , see again what we have already seen, in the spring we have to see what we have seen in the summer, we have to see the day that we have seen at night, with the sun where the first time it rained"

(José Saramago)

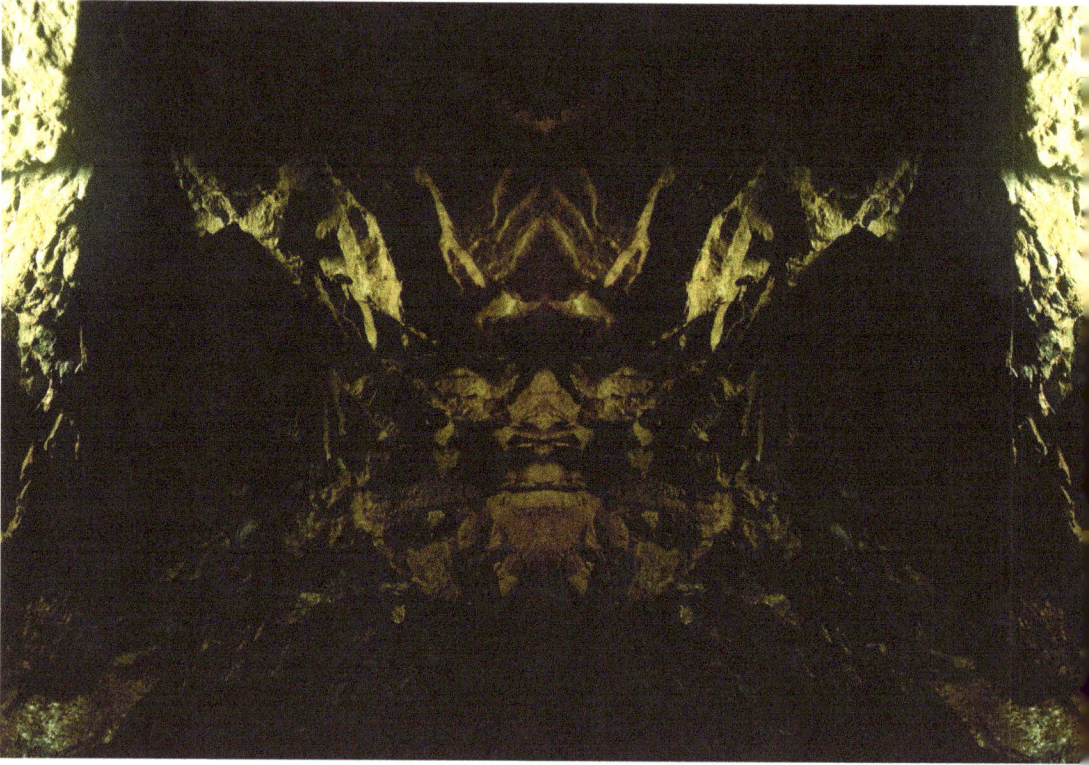

"*Eternal tourists of ourselves, there is no landscape but what we are. We possess nothing, for we don't even possess ourselves. We have nothing because we are nothing. What hand will I reach out, and to what universe? The universe isn't mine: it's me.*"

(Fernando Pessoa, *The Book of Disquiet*)

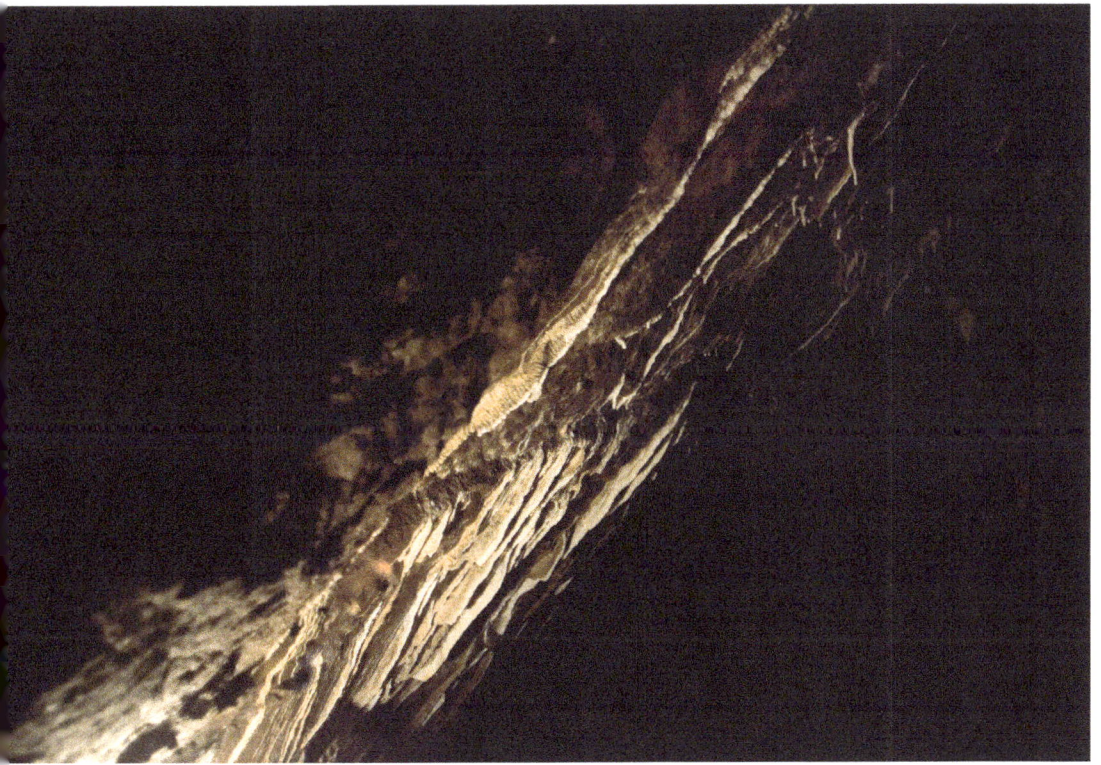

"*Man's real home is not a house, but the road, and that life itself is a journey to be walked on foot.*"

(Bruce Chatwin, *What Am I Doing Here ?*)

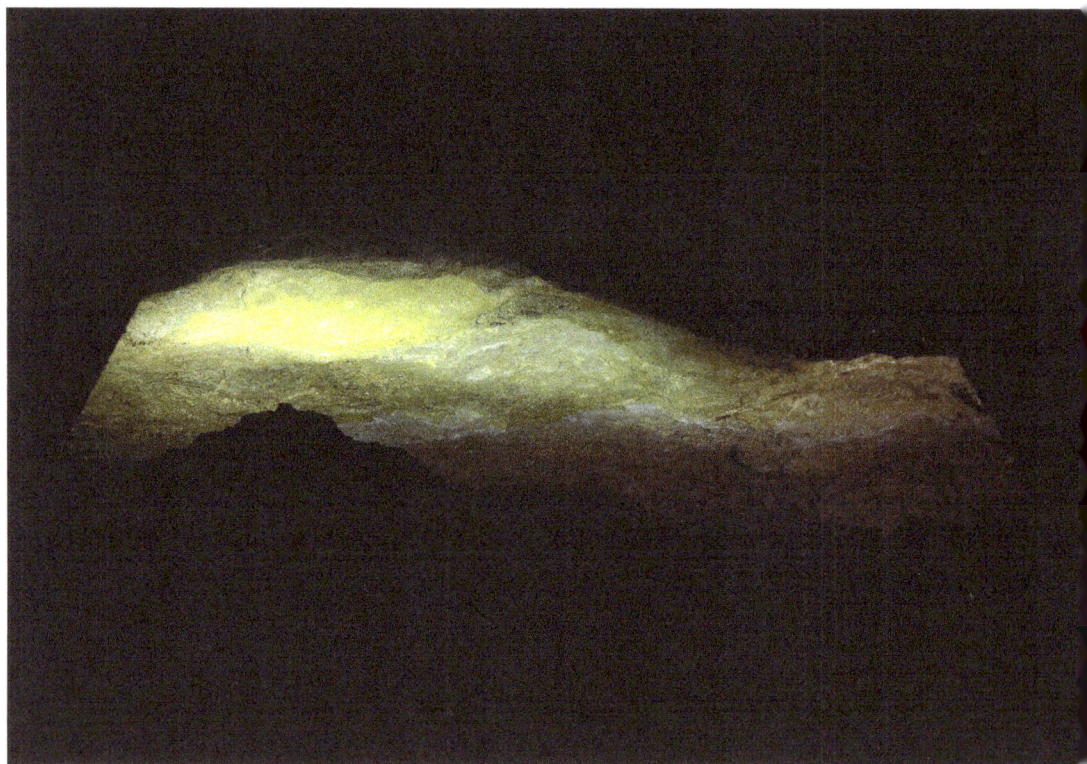

"Traveling far and wide to the world I met magnificent dreamers, men and women who stubbornly believe in dreams."

(Luis Sepulveda)

"To make the journey and not fall deeply in love, well, you haven't lived a life at all"

(William Parrish, *Meet Joe Black*)

"Paths are made by walking"

(Franz Kafka)

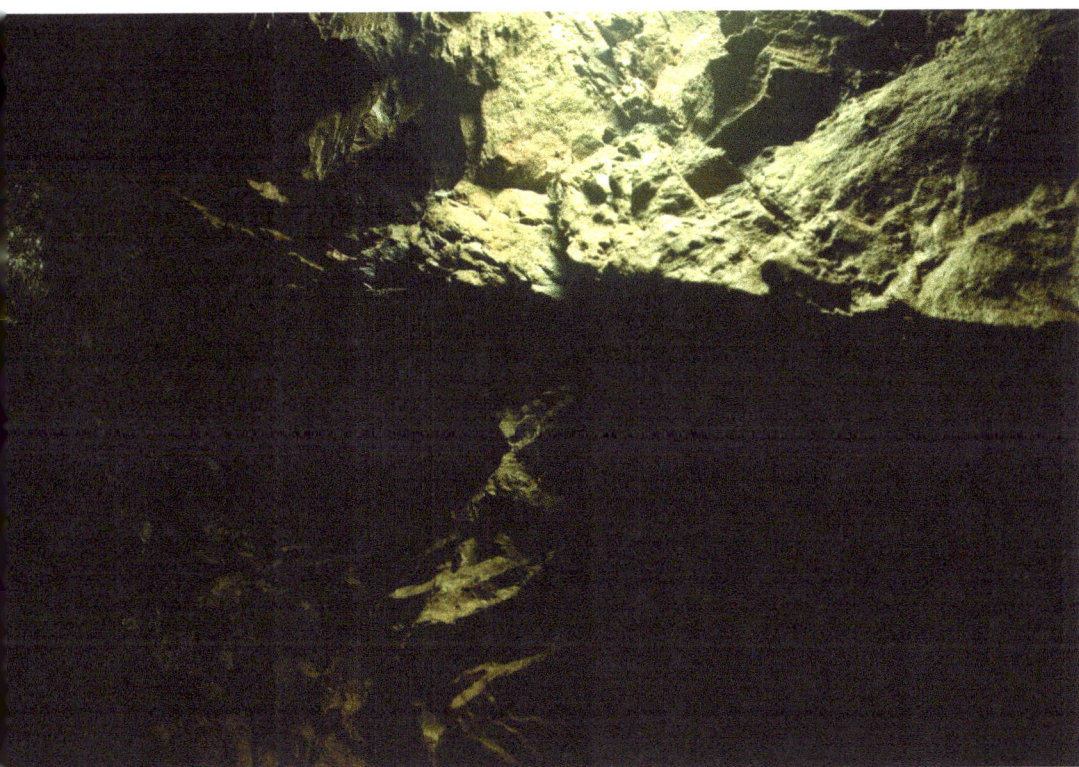

"*Direct your eye inward, and you'll find a thousand regions in your mind yet undiscovered. Travel them, and be expert in home-cosmography*"

(Henry David Thoreau)

"*Travel makes one modest. You see what a tiny place you occupy in the world*"

(Gustave Flaubert)

"I learned that sometimes a journey can take you to a place that is not on any map"

(Cold Fever, *movie*)

youcanprint

Finito di stampare nel mese di Novembre 2015
per conto di Youcanprint *self - publishing*

www.ingramcontent.com/pod-product-compliance
Lightning Source LLC
Chambersburg PA
CBHW061235150426
42812CB00055BA/2596